Finally, by paying special attention to the padded shape of the feet, you can refine your preliminary picture. Then you are ready to carefully erase the preliminary sketch.

The Head

Just as with the body, the head also should be sketched using ovals. Pay close attention to the eyes and the beak. These parts must be drawn in detail to correspond with the characteristic shape of each species.

Materials

- Pencil
- Eraser
- Colored pencils
- Black, fine-point felt-tip pen

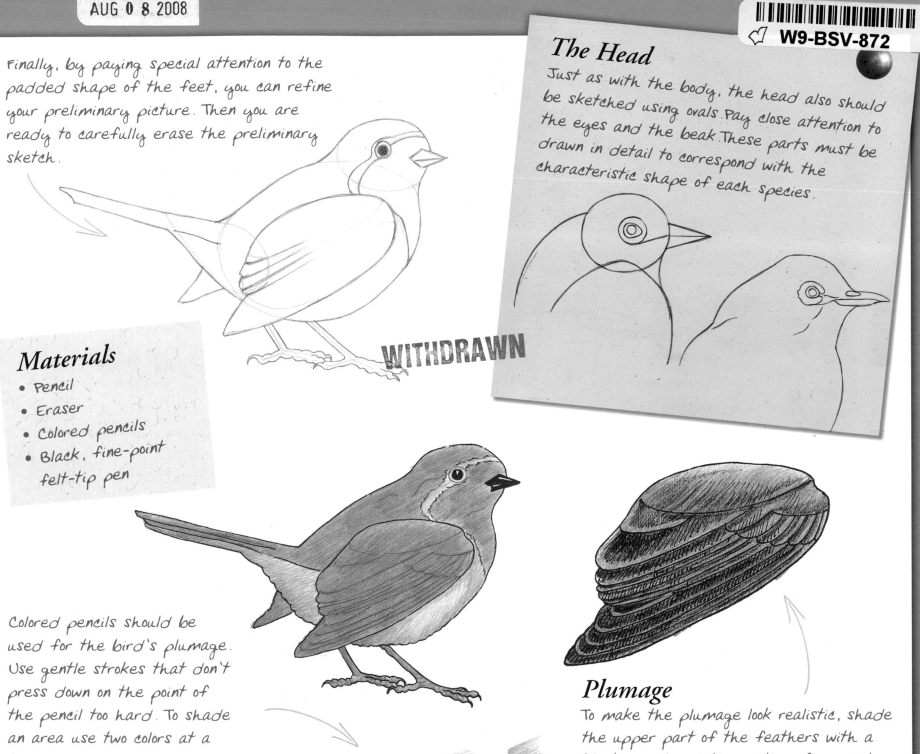

Colored pencils should be used for the bird's plumage. Use gentle strokes that don't press down on the point of the pencil too hard. To shade an area use two colors at a time.

Plumage

To make the plumage look realistic, shade the upper part of the feathers with a black pencil and then with a fine-point, felt-tip pen draw groups of fine lines over the part that has been colored.

FIELD GUIDES

Birds

Text by
Maria Angeles Julivert

ENCHANTED LION BOOKS
NEW YORK

First American Edition published in 2006 by
Enchanted Lion Books, 45 Main Street, Suite 519
Brooklyn, NY 11201

© 2005 Parramón Ediciones, S.A
Translation © 2006 Parramón Ediciones, S.A.

Conception and realization
Parramón Ediciones, S.A.

Editor
Lluís Borràs

Assistant Editor
Cristina Vilella

Text
Maria Àngels Julivert

Graphic design and layout
Estudi Toni Inglès

Photography
AGE-Fotostock, Boreal, Jordi Vidal, Prisma, Sincronia

Illustrations
Amadeu Blasco, Farrés il·lustració editorial.
Gabi Martin

Director of Production
Rafael Marfil

Production
Manel Sánchez

For information about permissions to reproduce
selections from this book, write to Permissions,
Enchanted Lion Books, 45 Main Street, Suite 519,
Brooklyn, NY 11201

A CIP record is on file with the Library of Congress

ISBN 1-59270-058-6

Printed in Spain

2 4 6 8 10 9 7 5 3 1

CONTENTS

A Marvelous World

Observing birds is one of the many rich activities we can enjoy in the natural world. The ease with which we can get close to them, though sometimes it will be with the help of binoculars, makes it possible for us to get into direct contact with nature itself. Their great variety of sizes, colors, songs or sounds, ways of flying, customs, and habitats form a marvelous source of delight as well as knowledge.

Since ancient times, people have been fascinated by birds and at times have even considered them sacred. Nevertheless, the relationship between humans and birds has always been contradictory. On the one hand, people have always admired birds, but on the other humans also have caused the disappearance of many species.

The aim of this guide is to bring the reader closer to the marvelous world of birds by offering guidelines for the best possible observation and sharing with the reader a knowledge of and respect for creatures whose existence is ever more at risk in today's world.

A Fantastic Show

To observe birds in their natural habitats is intriguing, rewarding and humbling. Even if one is not an expert, with a little patience, some study, and some luck, he or she will be able to identify some species. To do that it is important to pay close attention to the most significant characteristics of birds and to know something about their habits.

When we see a bird in flight we must look at its silhouette, notice how it flies, and observe the shape of its tail.

Be very careful

The spring is the best time to observe birds since it is when many of them are in their breeding period. But you must be careful not to disturb them because it is also when they are most vulnerable.

See them go by

The best time to observe the passage of migratory birds is usually between seven in the morning and one in the afternoon. In order to do so, it is best to find an elevated spot with good visibility on a clear day. Associations of naturalists and ornithologists can provide information on the best places to go.

Birds that we can find in a holm oak forest

1. European woodpecker
2. Eurasian jay
3. Golden oriole
4. Turtledove
5. Wren
6. Orphean warbler
7. Firecrest
8. Nightingale
9. Blackbird
10. Chaffinch
11. Great tit
12. Blue tit
13. Crested tit
14. Hoopoe

Wake up early

It is a good idea to start early, since in many places, such as marshes and lagoons, it is the first hour of the morning when you can see the most birds. In coastal areas, cultivated fields, parks and gardens, birds tend to be active all day long.

At dusk it is easy to see groups of birds flying to their roosts, where they rest for the night.

What to look for

It is essential to note the size, shape and color of the body, legs, beak, tail and wings, as well as any spots or special features the bird may have. Its voice and the type of habitat where we see it can also help us to determine which bird it is.

Birds everywhere

To observe birds in their natural environment, we can choose from a wide variety of places. Many birds live in woods and fields and also in the gardens in our cities.

The shape of a bird's body can give us an initial idea of the group to which it belongs. It is a good idea to note down as many features as possible.

Name

Shape

Size

Color

Wings

Tail

Feet, toes

Seen in

Date

Other notes

Advice:

• By planning your excursion you will have more chance of success.

• Do not talk loudly and move as quietly as possible

• Clothes should be in muted colors, and shoes should be comfortable

• If you are going into the country, you should take some food, something to drink, and a bag to put your trash iin.

• Do not bother the animals.

Don't be fooled

You have to keep in mind that the males and females of many different species have different coloring and sometimes vary in size as well. In these cases the male normally has the more striking plumage and the female is of a duller appearance.

The male grouse is very different from the female.

What Birds are Like

Birds are warm-blooded vertebrates, so their body temperature does not change with the temperature of their surroundings. They differ from other animals in having a body covered with feathers, a beak, and front legs that have turned into wings, though not all birds can fly. On the other hand, all birds lay eggs.

crown

neck

shoulder

wing

beak

throat

breast

thigh

tail

Feathers keep a bird's body warm.

tarsus

feet

toes

Because ducks spend a lot of time in water they have very oily feathers that don't get wet so that they remain able to fly.

Burma mallard

A very special skin

The skin of birds has almost no glands except for some at the base of the tail that are called uropygial glands and secrete a waterproof, oily fluid that they spread over their feathers. These glands are most highly developed in aquatic birds and are absent in some species such as parrots and pigeons.

A true mosaic of shapes and colors

9,000 different species of birds are known to exist. They live in the most diverse habitats, from oceans, forests and deserts to high mountains and even the frozen Arctic.

Incredible wings

The little hummingbird moves its wings 150 times per second and holds itself suspended in the air.

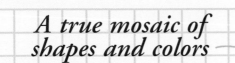

A great variety

The shape, color and size of birds is extremely varied. For example, while the male ostrich can grow to 7 1/2 feet tall and weigh as much as 350 pounds, the little Cuban hummingbird is scarcely 2 1/2 inches long and weighs less than an ounce.

The largest of all

The ostrich is the biggest bird in existence. Though it cannot fly, it is very fast. At its fastest it can move 120 miles per hour.

Hawfinch, in woods, fields, gardens and parks

Goshawk, in forests

Puffin, on seacoasts

Kingfisher, near rivers and clear water streams

Arctic Loon, in lakes

Purple Heron, in marshes, swamps and reedbeds

Golden Eagle, in mountainous areas

7

To Peck and Run

Birds obtain their nourishment with their beaks, which are formed by two corneous pieces that cover the bones of the mandibles. The type of beak a bird has reflects its diet. Similarly, because birds have different habitats and need to move over different types of ground or to swim, their feet vary greatly from species to species.

Taking measurements

To measure a bird's beak and head use the V-shaped part of a drawing compass. Next, compare the two lengths. This ratio helps to classify birds by the food they eat.

Beaks for all seasons

By examining the beaks of different birds we can determine what they eat and how they obtain their food. The sizes and shapes of beaks are extremely varied.

The beak of insect eating birds can be narrow and sharp (bee-eater) or wide (swallow)

swallow

bee-eater

The beak of small cranes is often long and narrow, like the beak of this avocet

avocet

Omnivorous birds tend to have thick, strong beaks (crow)

crow

Freshwater birds tend to have flat beaks (Northern Shoveler)

Northern shoveler

Birds that feed on grains and seeds tend to have strong beaks that are short and thick (common greenfinch)

common greenfinch

falcon

flamingo

pelican

Birds of prey have sharp, hooked beaks with cutting edges (peregrine falcon)

Some beaks are designed to filter water and capture algae and small plankton crustaceans (flamingo)

The very long, straight beak of the Pelican, with its upper part ending in a hook and a large bag hanging from the lower mandible, is unusual

Show me your foot

By looking at a bird's feet, we can deduce a lot about their customs and where they live.

Climbing birds like the imperial woodpecker have 4 toes, two in front and two in back, in order to hold onto and climb tree trunks. These feet are called, zygodactyl.

Birds that live in wetlands and marshy areas have very long, thin feet with toes that tend to be elongated. The jacana is an extreme case of this. With unusually long toes that also are spread to distribute its weight, it is able to walk on the leaves that float on the water.

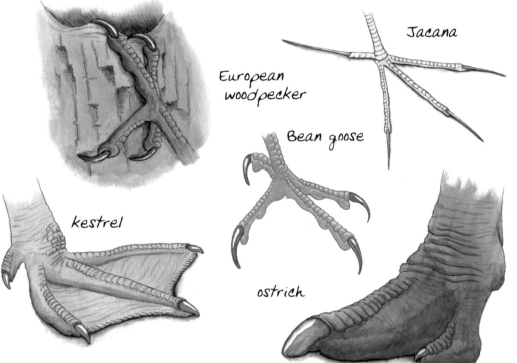

Jacana

European woodpecker

Bean goose

kestrel

ostrich

The webbed feet of aquatic birds have a membrane that joins the toes together, thereby permitting these birds to swim fast.

The feet of birds of prey are strong, with highly curved, sharp talons

Flightless birds like the ostrich have only 2 toes, which makes their feet ideal for walking and running.

Some birds, such as pigeons, parrots and diurnal birds of prey have a spot of bare skin at the base of the beak which is called a cere and can be brightly colored.

Zygodactyl foot of a tree-dwelling bird.

9

So many feet!

Most birds have scales covering part of their feet and legs and 4 toes, three pointed forward and a hind toe, the thumb, that points backward. The thumb is usually quite small and does not always rest on the ground. The middle toe generally is the longest. There also are birds that have three toes, and those of the ostrich family have only two.

A Coat of Lovely Colors

Feathers cover the skin of birds and are the equivalent of fur on mammals. There are feathers of many different types and sizes, as well as colors, and some of them are truly spectacular.

Changing Clothes

In time feathers wear out, so birds change them at least once a year, in a process called molting. Some birds, such as ducks, lose almost all their feathers at one time, and so for a while they are unable to fly. But the majority of birds change them gradually. The albatross, for example, can take as long as three years to shed all its feathers.

Winter livery

Summer livery

There are birds, such as the rock ptarmigan, that have different plumage in summer and winter

Similar but Different

The feathers that cover the bases of the longer main feathers of a bird's wings and tail are called coverts. They help to maintain body temperature and to protect from cold, sun and rain. The feathers on the wings, called remiges, are large and strong and make it possible for the bird to fly. The feathers on the tail are important for establishing direction during flight.

Retrices

Secondary remiges

Secondary coverts

Alula

Primary coverts

Primary remiges

What a Tail!

In some birds, like the peacock, the feathers of the tail are incredibly long, bright and colorful.

The feathers on the wings have different names -- primary, secondary and tertiary. The wing coverts, which are more delicate, cover the remiges. The alula is attached to the "thumb" and functions like the ailerons (moveable flaps) on the wings of an airplane. Tail feathers are called retrices, or steering feathers. Most birds have 12 (6 pairs).

What are Feathers Like?

A typical bird feather is made up of a quill or calamus, which is hollow and is inserted into the flesh, and the rachis, which is solid and flexible. On either side of the rachis are the barbs, which have in turn smaller filaments, the barbules, which are sometimes joined together by tiny hooklets, called barbicels..

Birds arrange their plumage with their beaks, untangling it and putting each feather in its place.

Feathers or Down?

Birds' feathers, which are hard and flexible, are actually modified scales. They are made of keratin, like the fur and horns of mammals. There are various types of feathers, namely: the down, mostly located on the lower part of the body; the filoplumes, threadlike hairs that grow between the feathers; and the penna or true feathers that cover a bird's body, wings and tail.

1. The down, soft and light, serves as insulation.
2. The filoplumes are like threads or fine, long hairs.
3. The penna or true feathers have different names depending on where they are located.
4. Rachis
5. Barbs
6. Barbules
7. Down
8. Quill or calamus

11

A Strong, Light Frame

For ornithologists, a birds' skull is a very useful element, since it makes species identification possible.

While a bird's skeleton is strong, it does not weigh much because the bones are very light. Some of the bones are even hollow (there is no marrow) and have air chambers. The majority of birds have a large keel on the breastbone which anchors the powerful muscles that move the wings in flight. The clavicles are joined at the front so that the two wings move together.

Vertebrae

The vertebrae on the neck are numerous and have a good deal of flexibility, but not all birds have the same number of cervical vertebrae. The vertebrae in the tail, on the other hand, have been reduced to only a few in all species.

The neck of the flamingo is long, thin and flexible

1. Jaws	5. Breastbone	9. Fibula	13. Keel	17. Cubitus
2. Cervical vertebrae	6. Ribs	10. Carpus-metacarpus	14. Tarsus-metatarsus	18. Radius
3. Clavicle	7. Scapula	11. Femur	15. Pygostyle	19. First digit
4. Coracoids	8. Tibia	12. Sacrum	16. Humerus	20. Second and third digit

Arms for Flying

The wings are the anterior limbs of the bird, equivalent to arms and hands. Most birds have only three "fingers" on their hands, which do not have claws.

Birds Were Not Always Like This

Birds are descended from reptiles. The first fossil of a bird's skeleton to be discovered was of the Archaeopteryx, a primitive bird about the size of a crow that looked like a reptile, and had the characteristics of both a reptile and a bird.

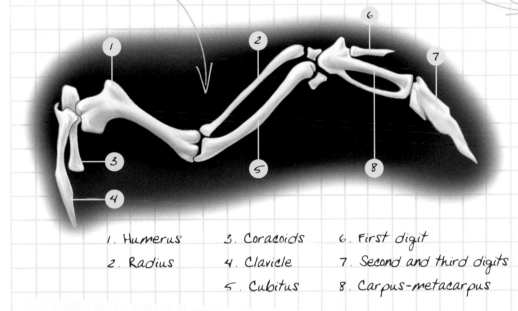

1. Humerus
2. Radius
3. Coracoids
4. Clavicle
5. Cubitus
6. First digit
7. Second and third digits
8. Carpus-metacarpus

The pectoral muscles contract and relax, making it possible for the wings to flap.

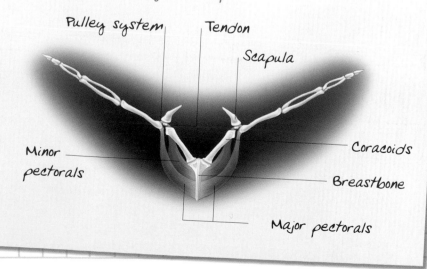

Pulley system
Tendon
Scapula
Coracoids
Minor pectorals
Breastbone
Major pectorals

A Jaw in the Shape of a Beak

The beak of a bird, which is the equivalent of the jaw in other animals, is covered with a corneous layer that renews itself as it is worn down by use. There are no teeth inside the beak, and the nasal cavities are at its base.

13

A Practical Organism

The internal organs of birds also are designed to lighten it's weight. Consequently, the sexual organs are very small and reproduction is oviparous, with eggs produced to hatch outside of the body. If female birds had to carry the embryo inside themselves flying would be difficult, even impossible.

Beating very fast

A bird's heart is very large and beats very fast. The smaller the bird the faster its heart beats. The heart is divided into two parts, right and left, and has two auricles and two ventricles.

Where does the food go?

The digestive system begins in the mouth. The food goes down the esophagus, which has a dilatation or sack - the crop - where food is stored and softened before going to the stomach. Birds have a glandular stomach, which produces gastric juices, and a grinding stomach - the gizzard. The intestine, which is elongated, digests and absorbs the food and ends in the rectum.

14

the esophagus is elongated

crop

the glandular stomach breaks down the food

liver

lungs

the gizzard grinds the food

intestines

both the reproductive and excretory systems open into the cloaca

A cool, ventilated body

Birds have two lungs that are not very large. Air reaches them through the larynx and the trachea. They also have small air chambers, called air sacs, which are connected to the lungs and penetrate their hollow bones and between some organs. The air sacs, which lighten the bird's weight, also work like ventilators in that they aid breathing and keep the body from getting too warm while flying.

The respiratory system is made up of the larynx, the trachea, the lungs and the air sacs. These are most numerous in birds that are strong flyers.

A canary's heart typically beats more than 500 times a minute.

cervical sac

lung

abdominal sac

interclavicular sac

anterior thoracic sac

posterior thoracic sac

Grinding food

The musculature of the gizzard of grain-eating birds is stronger and more highly developed than that of birds that feed on meat or fish because their food is harder and thus more difficult to grind up.

The woodpecker sticks his tongue into the hollows of trees to catch insects and other small invertebrates.

Let's look at the tongue

Birds' tongues are very flexible and not always the same. In parrots, for example, the tongue is thick, while woodpeckers have long, sticky tongues.

Saving water

The excretory system does not have a bladder. Birds eliminate uric acid instead of urea, so they require less water.

The Conquest of the Air

Instead of arms and hands, birds have wings covered with feathers. They also have an aerodynamic body, light hollow bones, and powerful chest muscles. It is on account of this particular make-up that most, though not all, birds can fly.

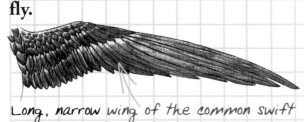

Long, narrow wing of the common swift

What are wings like?

Wings and tails vary in shape and size from one species to another depending on the type of life characteristic of the species. Some birds, like vultures and eagles which soar through the air, need to have a relatively large wing surface. Faster birds have thin, pointed wings with a surface that is small in relation to their weight.

Large, broad wing of the European buzzard

Silent flyers

Owls have broad wings and their feathers are soft, which means that their flight is quiet. Since they hunt by night they otherwise would frighten off their prey.

Taking off!

There are birds that have to pick up speed before they can take off. For that reason they start out running, while beating their wings. This is the case with many aquatic birds. Others take off from high places

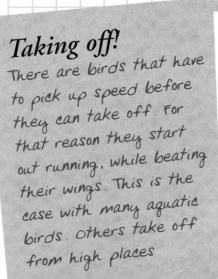

Landing

At the moment of alighting a bird has to brake. It does this by opening its tail, flapping its wings and straightening out its body vertically.

Ways of Flying

Wings make it possible for birds to stay in the air and move from place to place, while using the tail as a rudder. Although they generally propel themselves through the air by flapping their wings up and then down, not all birds fly in the same way.

Gliding flight is performed with the wings extended so that they flap very little. Diurnal birds of prey use ascending currents of hot air to soar up, as if they were flying on a hang-glider. Big seabirds, on the other hand, since there are no thermal currents over the sea, alternate between diving on the wind and using turns to gain altitude against the wind.

Flapping flight is most common among birds. Wings go regularly up and down at a greater or lesser speed. First, they beat their wings up and back, holding them lifted over their back. Next, the wings descend to a horizontal position, from which they go down and forward until they are situated in front of the head. Then the pattern starts all over again.

Diagram of the gliding flight of seabirds.

Diagram of the gliding flight of birds of prey.

When it dives down upon its prey, the peregrine falcon can travel over 175 miles per hour. It is a very agile and quick bird of prey.

Let's Eat!

Fruit, seeds, insects, worms and small vertebrates (such as lizards, rodents and fish) are some of the things birds eat. Some, like crows or ostriches, have quite a varied diet; you could say they eat everything. Others, however, have a more limited diet, such as the osprey, which feeds mostly on fish.

The osprey eats fish almost exclusively, catching them between its powerful talons.

White stork pellets are sticky and medium-sized (from 1 1/2-2 1/2 inches long and from 1-1 1/2 inches in diameter).

Pellets

Some birds, such as crows and owls, regurgitate the part of their food that they cannot digest – hair, feathers or bones – in the form of little bundles that are called "pellets." These are different for each species.

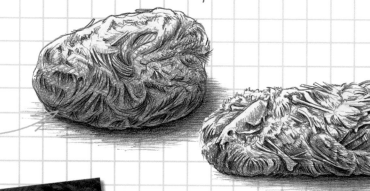

Eagle owl pellets are quite large (up to 6 inches long by 1 1/2 inches in diameter).

Stones for chewing

Birds do not chew their food since they have no teeth. To help grind up their food they often swallow small stones that act as millstones.

18

Strategies for survival

The ways in which birds obtain their food are almost as varied as their diet. Some birds fly or glide, scanning the area in search of food. Others remain still, waiting for their prey to come near. Razorbills, penguins and puffins dive for fish.

lammergeyer

penguin

Why do they do it?

The black stork and some cranes open their wings while fishing. We do not know exactly why, whether it is because making a shadow with their wings prevents reflection on the water or whether they do it to attract the attention of the fish.

Common crane fishing with extended wings.

This **acorn** has been pecked at by a great tit. This bird eats insects as well as fruit, berries and seeds.

19

Skill can be worth more than strength

The **lammergeyer** feeds on the bones of dead animals. When a bone is too big for it to swallow whole, the bird drops it down onto rocks from a great height in order to break it.

The **Egyptian vulture** has learned to break the hard shell of an ostrich egg by dropping a stone onto the egg.

The Art of Seduction

female frigate bird

male frigate bird

The majority of birds reproduce once a year, normally when weather conditions are conducive and the availability of food is good. During this period the males of many species display adornments of bright colors that they show off in front of the females.

Golden pheasant

The fighting ruff
The ruff of "fighting feathers" that males have on the neck during the reproduction period is not the same color in all species.

The male frigate bird puffs up the big sack on its neck, which is of a striking red color.

Between faithfulness and polygamy
There are birds that mate for life and get together every year with the same partner. There also are other birds that couple for only one season. Moreover, there are those, like the pheasant, that mate with several females. More unusual is the case of the quail where the females mate with several males.

Display of charms

When the breeding season begins each male occupies a specific territory, ranging in size from small to large, that he will defend against other males. Following this, the courtship rituals used to attract females to the chosen spot begin. These consist of a song or an exhibition of feathers, and offerings of food or branches are also frequent, as are dances, which may be extremely varied.

Some birds, such as the grebe, have very striking rituals. Males and females perform an elaborate dance on the water.

They approach one another, shaking their crests of feathers.

They submerge in the water. The female rises out of it with her neck stretched out while the male makes a kind of bow.

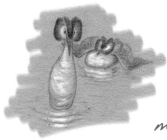

They bring their breasts together, rising up out of the water.

They collect water weeds with their beaks.

Getting together

Some species of birds come together during the breeding period to form large colonies, sometimes made up of thousands of couples.

The gardener birds of Guinea and Australia build platforms, arbors or towers with weeds, branches and leaves. Some species even decorate with brightly colored objects, such as small stones, pieces of vegetation, or even bits of plastic.

The male dances and struts in front of the female, inviting her to form a couple.

Home, Sweet Home

Birds show great ingenuity when it comes time to build the nest. The size and shape of the nest vary from one species to another. There are big ones, small ones, round ones, and even those that consist of large platforms. The nest can be bare or covered with different materials, such as moss, feathers, hair or even cobwebs.

The weaverbird's nest hangs from a branch and has a large, tube-shaped entrance at the bottom.

The most common nests have the form of a cup with a greater or lesser depth.

Anywhere will do

Nests can be situated in caves, holes, tree trunks, or even in abandoned buildings. There also are birds that prefer to nest in the open air, on either the ground, branches, high treetops, or even inaccessible cliffs.

The woodpecker tends to build its nest inside a tree trunk.

The kingfisher digs a tunnel leading into a chamber.

There are birds that do not build nests, but rather lay their eggs right on the ground or on a covering made up of a few branches.

In some species both the male and the female take part in building the nest.

In other species only one of the two does the whole job.

Megapodes build a little pile of leaves, branches and other vegetation, where they bury their eggs, which incubate in the warmth generated by the decomposition of the vegetation and the heat of the sun.

Bigger and bigger

There are birds such as the stork and the bald eagle that use the same nest year after year, rebuilding and enlarging it every season. These nests can become extraordinarily large. The majority of birds, however, make a new nest each year.

23

Anything will do

The materials used in the construction of the nest are quite varied. Simple, rudimentary nests are made from branches, weeds, dirt or clay. More elaborate constructions are made from branches and other materials that are woven together.

The crag martin makes its nest with balls of clay in the form of a pot.

The tailorbird (belonging to the warbler family) sews the edges of leaves together with plant fibers to form a sack

The sociable weavers construct a big group nest where several couples nest, and each couple has its individual place and entrance.

The structure of the penduline tit's nest is made of branches, and then covered with fibers, wool, cotton, hair or cobwebs.

Variety is the Name of the Game

Eggs, which may be oval, elongated, round or pear-shaped, have varied coloring, and many are spotted. The number of eggs laid by a bird each year ranges from a single one, as in the case of the albatross, to more than 20 in other species.

Partridge brooding eggs.

Eggs have a thick calcareous shell that protects the embryo.

A job for everyone

In many cases it is the female that takes charge of incubating the eggs, but the males of some birds also participate in the job. In some species it is only the male that takes care of incubation. Incubation time varies from one species to another, from a few days to several weeks or even months.

Egg of the black-winged stilt

Egg of the European nightjar

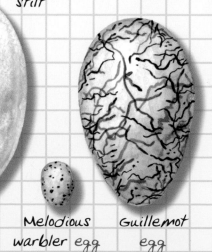

Breaking the shell

Chicks break out of their shells, which become thinner toward the end of the incubation period, by using a hard bump on the point of their beaks, called the egg tooth. They lose this shortly after birth.

Pelican egg

Melodious warbler egg

Guillemot egg

Nidiculous chicks

The young of some birds are born completely defense-less, with eyes closed, no feathers, very little down, and no ability to fly. These are called nidiculous and they are totally dependent on their parents.

The quicker ones

Nidifugous chicks, on the other hand, are more precocious and quickly learn to take care of themselves. They are born with their eyes open and their bodies covered with a thick down, and they leave the nest shortly after birth, though they tend to stay with their parents for a while.

The young of the golden plover are nidifugous.

Many birds feed their young by regurgitating predigested food into the chick's mouth. Others, like birds of prey, cut the food into pieces before giving it to their young.

Pigeons secrete milk from their crop which they give to their chicks directly from the mouth.

Sparrow hawks feed their chicks.

The seagull's chicks peck at the red spot on each parent's beak to ask for food.

The meadow pipit feeds its chicks on insects.

The brood patch

The majority of birds have a special area on the abdomen called the brood patch, which they put over their eggs. This area gives off a lot of heat. It only appears during the breeding period and is an area of bare skin that is highly irrigated with blood. An unusual case is that of the masked booby, which incubates its single egg between its feet, while covering its egg with a fold of skin. This is a unique case among birds.

Young feathers

Before reaching adulthood, chicks go through a juvenile phase in which they have changed the plumage they had when they were very young, but they still do not have the same plumage as that of an adult bird. This often makes it possible for us to distinguish a bird as a juvenile, even though it already is almost the same size and weight as its parents.

The cuckoo, famous for its brood parasitism, puts its eggs singly into the nests of other birds that usually will care for the baby cuckoo even at the expense of its own chicks. The host bird seems to allow for this because over time cuckoos have developed char-acteristics that work to mislead other birds. But not all birds are fooled!

Alert at Every Moment

Communication is an indispensable aspect of a bird's life, whether it is used to seek a mate, relate to one another, or warn of some danger. In addition to the voice, or call, various senses, especially sight and hearing, also play an important role in communication, as well as in many other aspects of a bird's life.

Birds' eyes have limited mobility. That is why birds constantly move their heads.

Of all birds, diurnal raptors are the ones that have the best eyesight. The eagle can see animals the size of a field mouse while flying very high.

I smell food

In general, birds do not have an excellent sense of smell, except in those species that depend on smell to find their food. In most cases, the nasal orifices are at the base of the beak.

Knowing how to listen

Birds' hearing is very highly developed, particularly in night birds. Oilbirds, for example, nest in caves and depend on their hearing to fly in the dark. These birds make sounds that they can detect with their fine sense of hearing when they bounce off the walls.

These sounds are not high frequency since birds are unable to hear ultrasounds.

The kiwi is a nocturnal bird that finds its food under fallen leaves thanks to its acute sense of smell. Uncharacteristically, it has nostrils at the tip of its beak.

Look what my eyes are like!

The sense of sight is very highly developed in birds, and, like us, they can see colors. Their angle of vision depends on the position of their eyes. In most birds the eyes are situated on the sides of the head. Birds' eyes are protected by eyelids and by a transparent membrane, the nictitating membrane.

The more centered the eyes, the better stereoscopic vision and long-range vision both are, but the smaller the visual field that the eyes can cover.

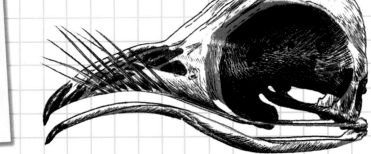

Sparrow

Eurasian woodcock

Owl

Sound is produced when air passes the membranes.

The sense of touch

The sense of touch, which is of little importance for birds, is usually located in the tongue, the beak, the nostrils, or around the eyes.

The vibrissae are like fine hairs with a touch function.

Little tenors

Birds have an extensive repertoire of sounds that range from cries, howls, squawks or clicks to the melodious singing of some birds.

The nightingale emits a great variety of calls and different notes.

"Talking" with sound

Birds emit sounds to defend their territory, communicate with their mate or young, and to sound an alarm. Not all of them sing, however. The syrinx is the organ that makes the sounds that birds make possible. It is located at the end of the trachea, just where it divides to form the bronchi.

Tireless Travelers

Every year migratory birds make a round trip between the place where they were born and the place where they spend the winter, sometimes covering incredible distances. Other birds, in contrast, are sedentary and stay in the same place all year round. There also are species that can be migratory or sedentary, depending on the area in which they live.

Expert navigators

There are birds, such as swifts, that migrate by day, using the position of the sun to orient themselves. Others, like the cuckoo, prefer to travel by night, guided by the stars. Yet others, such as ducks, migrate both day and night. The earth's magnetic field and features of the landscape such as mountains and rivers help them to gain their orientation.

Taking on fuel

Before setting off on their long journey, birds, in addition to molting their feathers, devote themselves to eating a lot, thereby accumulating a large amount of fat, which they use as reserve nourishment. There are species, such as the sparrow hawk, that will not eat again until reaching its destination, while others make short stops to eat.

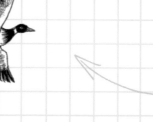

V formation typical of many birds, such as ducks.

Forming a squadron

Flying involves a great expenditure of energy, so many birds travel in flocks. This is a way of saving energy since it helps to reduce wind resistance. There also are birds that travel alone, such as the golden oriole.

Route maps

Most migratory birds begin their trip to warmer climates at summer's end or in the autumn and return to breeding and nesting areas in early spring or shortly before. They often follow the same routes both coming and going. Migratory routes tend to follow the course of rivers, mountain ranges and coastlines.

The most usual **migratory** routes go from the northern to the southern hemisphere, but there also are those that go from east to west.

The **arctic tern** spends summers in Greenland and Alaska and in June commences an immensely long journey that will take it to Chile and even to Antarctica. In total it travels more than 10,550 miles on its outward journey alone.

We Want to Fly!

Birds are continually confronted by different dangers. Their natural enemies are the animals that feed not only on adult specimens, but also on their eggs and their young. However, it is above all humans who are a bird's worst enemy, despite the great benefits we obtain from birds. This is because birds have no defense against the human actions that threaten their well-being.

A Skilled Hunter

Since long ago humans have taken advantage of the falcon's skill in hunting, training them to bring back their captured prey.

Easy Prey

The natural predators of birds include some mammals and reptiles as well as other birds.

Eggs and chicks are succulent morsels for many snakes.

Unselfish Helpers

Birds serve to benefit human beings in numerous ways. Apart from providing us with food, birds control the population of certain animals that are harmful to our crops, such as insects and small rodents. Birds that live on carrion also are useful, since they clear the environment of dead bodies.

Many birds are raised on farms to provide us with meat and eggs.

Danger Everywhere

Pesticides, traps, environmental pollution, the destruction of habitats, poaching, illegal traffic in eggs and electrical cables are some of the reasons why certain species of birds are seriously threatened today, or even in danger of extinction.

The imperial eagle and the black stork are two species in grave danger. Their numbers have been decreasing year by year and now only a few remain.

Dyed Black

Oil spilled at sea sticks to the feathers of seabirds, preventing them from flying and causing their death.

There is Still Hope

Fortunately, we are becoming more and more aware of the need to protect the marvelous birds of our world, and many groups and societies are taking steps to do so. Laws have been passed to protect natural species, and organizations devoted to the protection and conservation of birds are becoming more and more numerous. Additionally, all over the world there now are places focused on preservation and on building up the populations of threatened species.

We still have time to save many species of birds, though for others it is already too late.

Artificial nests are manufactured to promote bird reproduction.

31

The links that exist between the orders shown below are not systematic. Rather, they refer to common traits that many of the species of the given order display, such as diet, habitat or habits.

SUPERORDER PALEOGNATHAE

Struthioniformes Ostrich

Rheiformes Ñandu nandu

Casuariformes Cassowary, Emu

Apterygiformes Kiwi

Tinamiformes Tinamou

SUPERORDER IMPENNES

Sphenisciformes Booby or penguin

SUPERORDER NEOGNATHAE

Gaviformes Loon

Podicepediformes Grebe

Procellariformes Albatross

Pelicaniformes Pelican, Frigatebird, Cormorant

Ciconiiformes Stork, Heron, Bittern

Phoenicopteriformes Flamingo

Anseriformes Duck, Swan, Goose

Falconiformes Falcon, Eagle, Vulture

Galliformes Turkey, Pheasant, Quail

Gruiformes Crane, Bustard, Coot

Charadriformes Tern, Gull, Avocet

Columbiformes Pigeon, Dove

Cuculiformes Cuckoo

Psittaciformes Parrot, Macaw, Cockatoo

Strigiformes Owl, Barn owl

Caprimulgiformes Nightjar, Oilbird

Trogoniformes Trogon

Coliformes Mousebird

Apodiformes Swift, Hummingbird

Coraciformes Kingfisher, Hoopoe, Bee-eater

Piciformes Imperial Woodpecker, Toucan

Passeriformes Lark, Blackbird, Swallow, Goldfinch, Crow, Magpie

Index

What do we need for bird watching?

Going out to watch birds can be fun and educational. By using this book and making observations in the field, you can begin the process of becoming an expert naturalist.

A digital camera with 6 magnifications will provide a good range. Pictures can either be printed at the lab, or from a computer.

A field guide will help you to identify the birds you see.

Colored pencils help to capture details of interest. Make sure to bring an eraser and a pencil sharpener.

A good pair of binoculars— minimum of 8 x 30 (magnification x diameter) is essential. **Be careful** not to focus on the sun!